ALTERNATOR BOOKS™

NATIVE LANDS AND SACRED PLACES

Reclaiming and Protecting Native Lands

CAYLA BELLANGER DEGROAT

Lerner Publications ◆ Minneapolis

Content consultant: Jill Doerfler

Lerner Publications Company
An imprint of Lerner Publishing Group, Inc.
241 First Avenue North
Minneapolis, MN 55401 USA

For reading levels and more information, look up this title at www.lernerbooks.com.

Main body text set in Aptifer Sans LT Pro Medium.
Typeface provided by Linotype AG.

Designer: Athena Currier
Lerner team: Sue Marquis

Map illustration on page 14 by Laura K. Westlund.

Library of Congress Cataloging-in-Publication Data

Names: DeGroat, Cayla Bellanger, author.
Title: Native lands and sacred places : reclaiming and protecting native lands / Cayla Bellanger DeGroat.
Description: Minneapolis, MN : Lerner Publications , [2025] | Series: Native rights (Alternator Books) | Includes bibliographical references and index. | Audience: Ages 8–12 | Audience: Grades 4–6 | Summary: "For Native American nations, land is sacred. Readers learn about the importance of sacred sites. They also discover how Native peoples are reclaiming their ancestral lands with the Land Back movement"— Provided by publisher.
Identifiers: LCCN 2024015000 (print) | LCCN 2024015001 (ebook) | ISBN 9798765646922 (lib. bdg.) | ISBN 9798765661710 (pbk.) | ISBN 9798765656754 (epub)
Subjects: LCSH: Indians of North America—Religion—Juvenile literature. | Sacred space—United States—Juvenile literature. | Indians of North America—Land tenure—United States—Juvenile literature. | Indians of North America—Reparations—Juvenile literature.
Classification: LCC E98.R3 D426 2025 (print) | LCC E98.R3 (ebook) | DDC 299.7/135—dc23/eng/20240411

LC record available at https://lccn.loc.gov/2024015000
LC ebook record available at https://lccn.loc.gov/2024015001

Manufactured in the United States of America
1-1010987-53133-5/30/2024

TABLE OF CONTENTS

INTRODUCTION
BEAR LODGE

Every June, Native American peoples gather at Bear Lodge in Wyoming's Black Hills. In the warm, summer sun, they hold ceremonies such as sweat lodges or the sun dance. The branches of trees are dotted with color from prayer ties, small bundles of sacred plants wrapped in colorful cloth.

For generations Bear Lodge, called Mato Tipila in Lakota, has been a sacred place for Great Plains tribes such as the Lakota, Cheyenne, Shoshone, and Kiowa. It is an important part of their spiritual beliefs and history.

Bear Lodge is estimated to be fifty million years old. This rock formation began as a pool of magma. The magma pushed up through the ground and cooled over millions of years. Over time, the rock around the cooled magma crumbled, revealing the 867-foot (264 m) Bear Lodge.

Bear Lodge is also called Devil's Tower. It is in Devil's Tower National Monument in Wyoming's Black Hills.

vital part of their spiritual beliefs and how they connect with the land and one another. Native Americans have the right to religious freedom. But that wasn't always true.

Prayer ties and offerings hang from a tree at Bear Lodge in 2009.

CHAPTER 1
Land and Spiritual Beliefs

Land is important to everyone. It's where we all live, eat, sleep, play, learn, and work. For Native nations and peoples, land is sacred. This means that land is a valued and respected part of their spiritual and religious beliefs.

Sacred Sites Are Sacred Places

Certain places may also be sacred sites. These sacred sites may be old or new and have different uses or meanings.

The Ocmuglee Mounds is a Muscogee burial site and is sacred to the nation.

Some sacred sites include burial sites, places for ceremonies, and areas where plants used for physical and spiritual medicines grow. Sacred sites may be connected to a tribe's religious beliefs through stories or historical events.

Chimney Rock is a sacred site for the Pueblo nation.

How do you know if something is sacred? What does the word *sacred* mean to you?

In modern times, the US has control of many Native sacred sites. Some of these are well-known such as Bear Lodge, and Chimney Rock in Arizona. These sites draw many non-Native tourists who enjoy the beauty of the sites but rarely have a spiritual connection to the area. Other sacred sites have been kept secret to better preserve and protect them from outsiders.

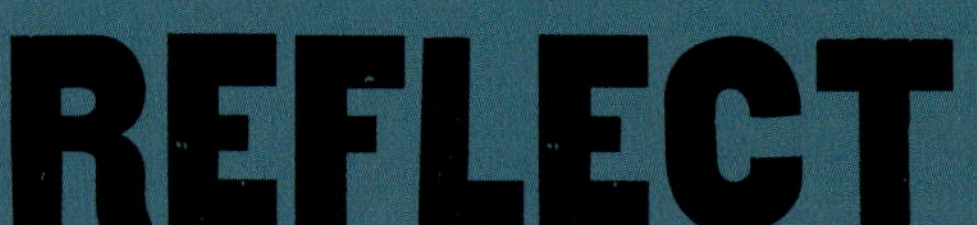

REFLECT

Are there any places that are very important to you or your family? What makes them important? Have you ever been able to visit those places? How do you feel when you visit those places?

From time immemorial, Native peoples cared for sacred sites and visited sacred sites whenever they needed. After European settlers arrived and forced Native nations from their lands, many Native peoples were cut off from these sacred places. Native peoples lost important knowledge of countless sacred places and histories, though they are working to preserve and renew what is left.

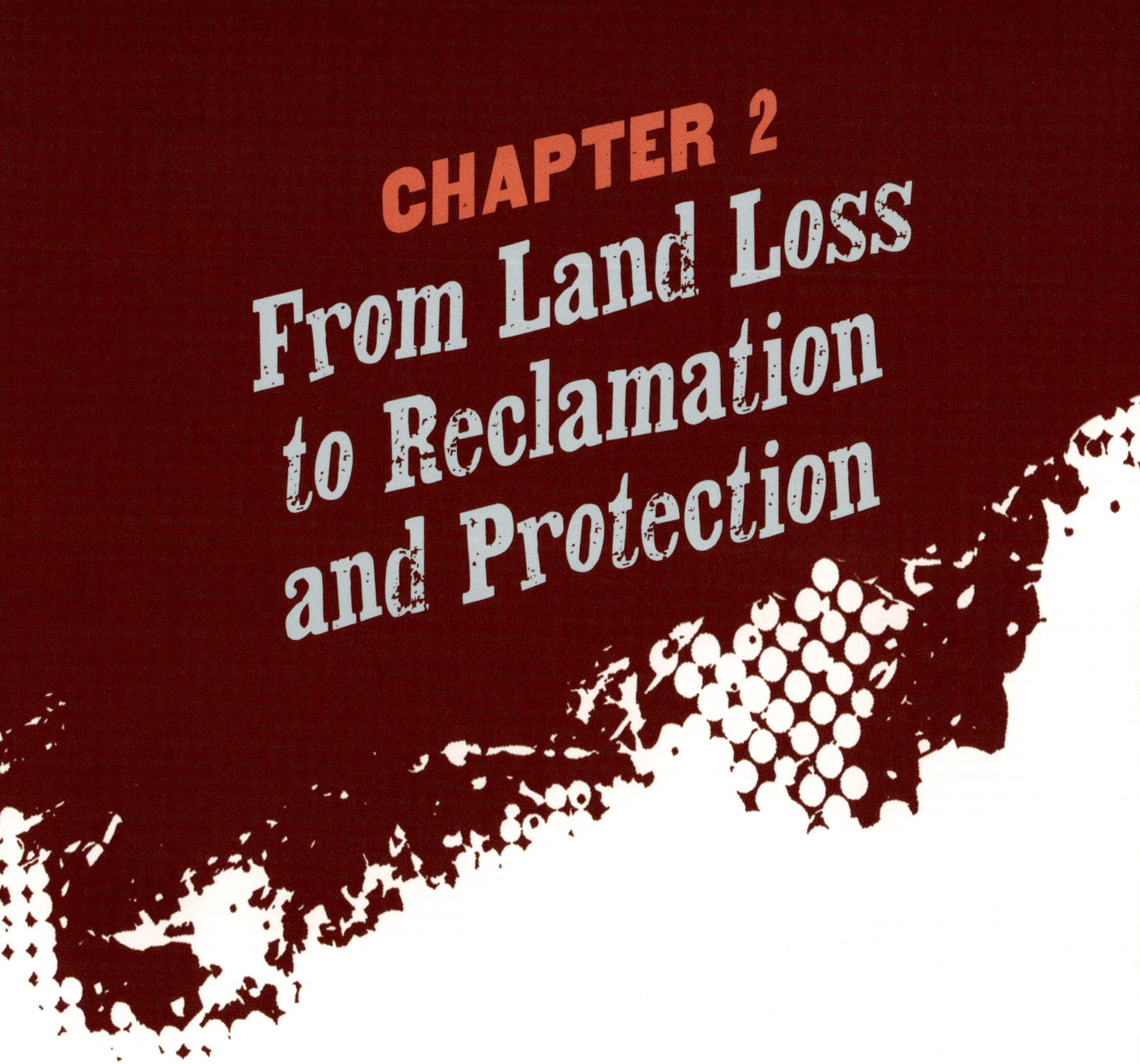

CHAPTER 2 From Land Loss to Reclamation and Protection

In the 1400s, European settlers began arriving on the land that is now the US. The North American continent was occupied by many different groups of Indigenous nations and peoples who had lived there for generations. Their lives and societies developed around the land and natural environment. They cared for and respected the land, which allowed them to survive and grow.

Rock art likely created by Shoshone people thousands of years ago

Settlers and Lands Lost

Life for Native American peoples changed dramatically as European settlements took over more land. Settlers brought with them the belief that land belonged to individuals and that it was something to be used. Native American spiritual beliefs say land is sacred. That means land should always be treated with respect.

European settlers also brought a lot of diseases and wars to North America. From 1490 to 1600, fifty-six million Indigenous North, Central, and South Americans died.

As more settlers arrived, more tribal nations were pushed from their original homelands.

They were also pressured to give up more and more of their land. The results were devastating. Research has found that by 2021 Native American tribes no longer had control of 99 percent of their lands.

European nations, and later the US government, made treaties, or formal agreements, with Native American tribes. Many of these treaties sold Native American lands to the other nations such as the US. Often Native American tribes kept a small portion of land to continue living on.

By 1700 there were 260,000 British settlers on the land that is now the US.

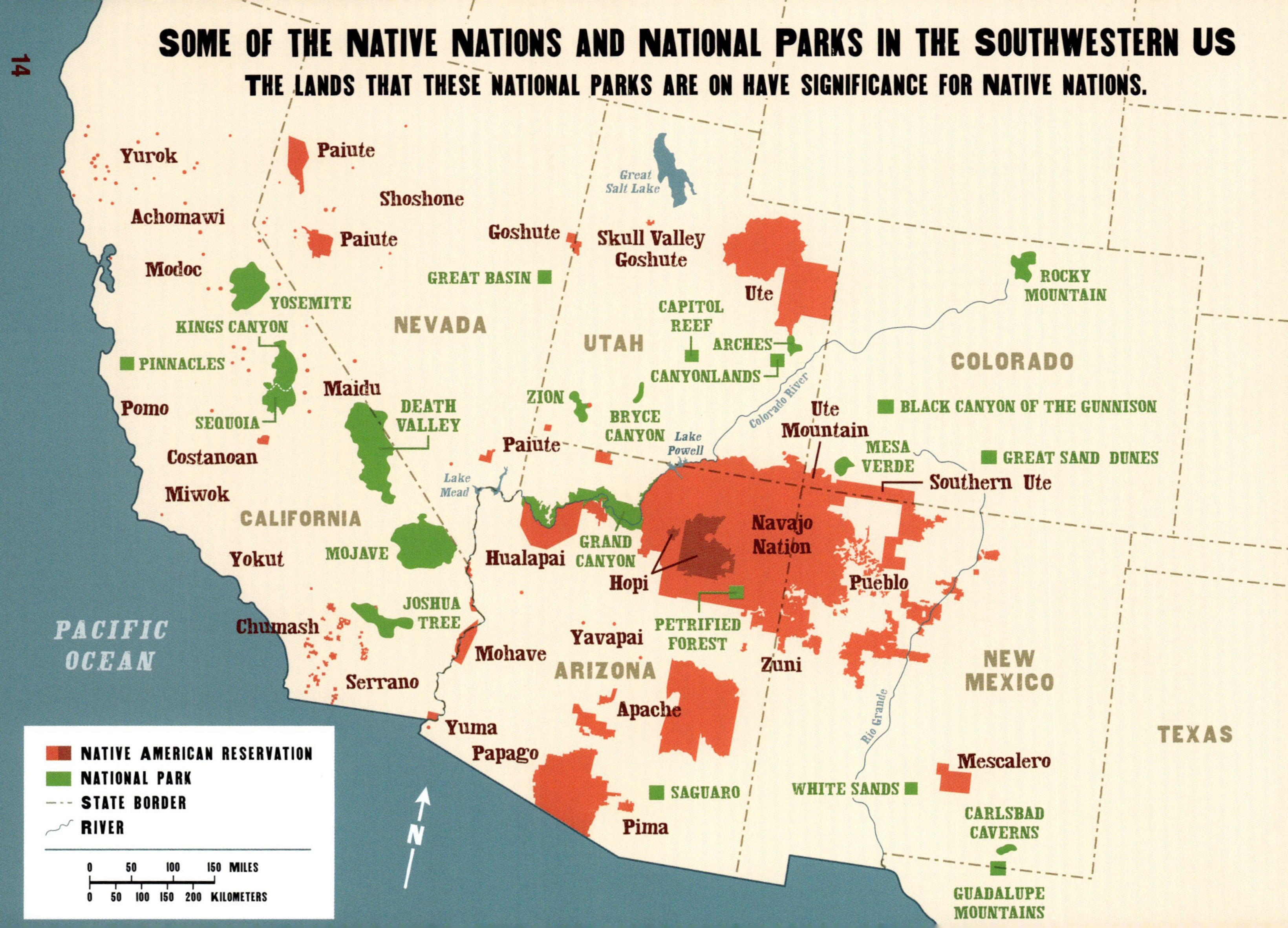
SOME OF THE NATIVE NATIONS AND NATIONAL PARKS IN THE SOUTHWESTERN US
THE LANDS THAT THESE NATIONAL PARKS ARE ON HAVE SIGNIFICANCE FOR NATIVE NATIONS.
Yurok
Paiute
Shoshone
Achomawi
Paiute
Goshute
Skull Valley Goshute
Great Salt Lake
Modoc
GREAT BASIN
YOSEMITE
KINGS CANYON
NEVADA
UTAH
Ute
CAPITOL REEF
ARCHES
CANYONLANDS
ROCKY MOUNTAIN
COLORADO
PINNACLES
Maidu
Pomo
SEQUOIA
DEATH VALLEY
ZION
BRYCE CANYON
Colorado River
Ute Mountain
BLACK CANYON OF THE GUNNISON
Paiute
Lake Powell
MESA VERDE
GREAT SAND DUNES
Southern Ute
Costanoan
Lake Mead
Miwok
CALIFORNIA
Navajo Nation
Hualapai
GRAND CANYON
Hopi
Yokut
MOJAVE
Pueblo
JOSHUA TREE
PETRIFIED FOREST
PACIFIC OCEAN
Chumash
Yavapai
Mohave
ARIZONA
Zuni
NEW MEXICO
Serrano
Apache
Rio Grande
Yuma
TEXAS
Papago
Mescalero
SAGUARO
WHITE SANDS
Pima
CARLSBAD CAVERNS
GUADALUPE MOUNTAINS
N
NATIVE AMERICAN RESERVATION
NATIONAL PARK
STATE BORDER
RIVER
0 50 100 150 MILES
0 50 100 150 200 KILOMETERS

The Sioux nation and the US sign an 1868 treaty that sets up a reservation.

The US often promised food, education, and medical care to Native nations in treaties. This was because without land and its abundant resources for life, living conditions were poor for Native nations. These treaties were often deceptive and the US often didn't fulfill its promises.

The Reservation Era

In the 1800s, the US government began forming reservations for tribes to live on. During the Reservation Era (1850–1887), some Native nations were forced to move to land reserved for them. These were tiny plots compared to the large ancestral lands they used to live on and needed for their way of life.

Life on reservations was hard. These lands didn't have the foods and medicines that Native American peoples had relied on for thousands of years. Other Native nations remained on small portions of land that they never sold.

Reservations isolated Native peoples. The US did not allow most people to travel or leave. They were mostly blocked from the land they traditionally used for hunting, gathering, or holding ceremonies. Those places were being used for white settlements.

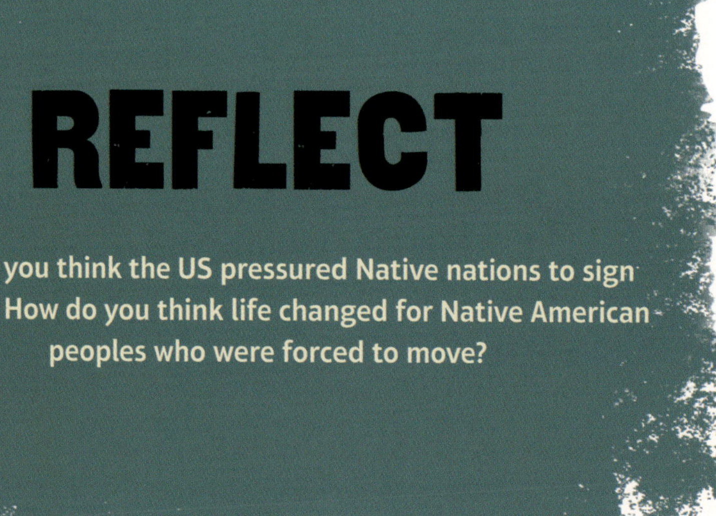

REFLECT

Why do you think the US pressured Native nations to sign treaties? How do you think life changed for Native American peoples who were forced to move?

Native children were forced to work and assimilate at boarding schools.

Forcing Native peoples off their lands was part of the US government's plan to assimilate them. Children were also taken from their families and forced to live at boarding schools where they were often abused and made to live as white Americans. Cut off from sacred sites, Native Americans could not protect or access these important places.

During the Reservation Era, sacred sites needed more protection than ever. Sacred sites, burial sites, and places where ancient peoples left behind objects from their lives were dug up by non-Native collectors. These collectors were often wealthy white people who did not have permission to take the objects. They looted sacred sites for objects like jewelry and pottery and desecrated burial sites by digging up human skeletons.

A Native American headdress displayed at a museum in Spain

They sold these stolen objects and ancestral remains to other private collectors or museums, who kept them and displayed them. Many museums became well known and wealthy because of their collections of looted ancestral remains and sacred objects.

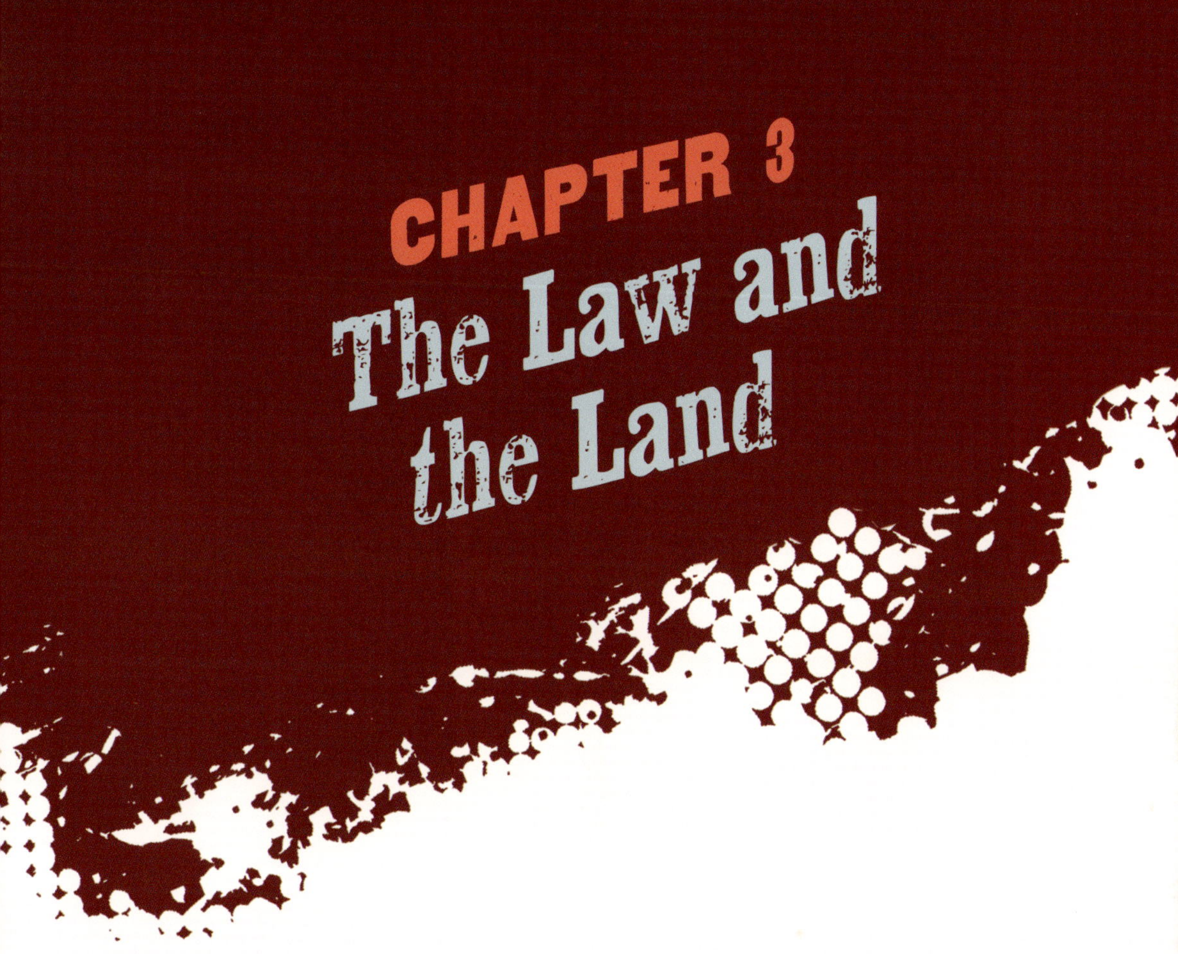

CHAPTER 3 The Law and the Land

In the 1900s, the US paid more attention to preserving certain cultural and natural resources on land it owned. President Theodore Roosevelt signed the Antiquities Act in 1906. It made rules about who could perform archaeological excavations.

It also gave the president the power to create national monuments. That year Bear Lodge became the US's first national monument. While this sacred site was protected, it would be a long time before a law protected the religious freedom of Native Americans.

Have you ever visited a national park or national monument? Do you know about the history of Native peoples who lived there?

Trust Responsibility

In the 1900s, several federal laws and policies began to protect Native American lands and sacred sites. These laws built on the trust responsibility. This is a special relationship between the US and Native nations.

The trust responsibility means the US government has a duty to protect treaty rights and land. It is a way that the government shows how important Native American lands are to the US.

The American Indian Religious Freedom Act of 1978 and the Religious Freedom Restoration Act of 1993 were passed to protect Native religious expression. But after legal challenges and court rulings, they did not give Native Americans much protection. Other laws made rules on how the government works with Native nations to protect sacred sites and gave the nations a bigger role in identifying and protecting sacred sites.

CALIFORNIA NATIVE AMERICAN HERITAGE COMMISSION

The logo of the California Native American Heritage Commission

The California Native American Heritage Commission was created in 1976 to advocate for Native American spiritual freedom. The commission created a system to identify and catalog sacred sites. It also made rules that protected sacred sites and Native Americans' right to religious expression.

Native and non-Native people protest to protect various freedoms in 2023.

Protecting and Preserving What Is Sacred

After many years of advocating for change, in 1990 the Native American Graves Protection and Repatriation Act (NAGPRA) was passed. It protects and preserves ancestral burial sites and other places and objects that Native American peoples hold sacred. NAGPRA continued the work the Native American Heritage Commission started.

NAGPRA forced US museums to make lists of the sacred Native American objects and ancestral remains they had. This gave Native nations a way to repatriate, or get back, objects and ancestral remains from museums. NAGPRA also gave tribes a way to protect any new discoveries.

A citizen of the Kumeyaay nation visits a cemetery in 2020.

The National Park Service manages the NAGPRA program and is also a major part of how the US manages the important land and sites it owns. The Bureau of Land Management and Bureau of Indian Affairs are also responsible for taking care of federally owned land. All the

Dr. Rosita Worl, a citizen of the Tlingit nation, talks about the importance of NAGPRA in 2013.

Parts of a thousand-year-old Pueblo building that's in the Grand Canyon National Park

land they manage was once home to hundreds of Native American tribes.

Native nations are advocating for the return of some land owned by the US government. Their goals are to get back traditional lands or to work together with the US to better protect and respect the land.

CHAPTER 4
Present and Future of Sacred Lands

Native nations continue to be land stewards. Some lands are being returned to them. The Land Back movement works to return stolen lands to Native nations. When tribes get back their ancestral lands, they are getting back a connection to their histories and traditions.

A citizen of the Robinson Rancheria Band of Pomo Indians smells a plant while deciding where to do a cultural burn in 2021.

Native American spiritual beliefs and the way they lived focus on the land being sacred. Over thousands of years living on the land that is now the US, Indigenous peoples cared for the land.

Citizens of the Nansemond nation celebrate Indigenous Peoples' Day in 2021.

RETURNING CROSS SWAMP

The Indigenous people of the Nansemond Nation lived on what is called Cross Swamp, an area along the Nansemond River, for thousands of years. In the 1600s, European settlers forced them from the land.

The Nansemond nation split up and many Nansemond people moved west. Some Nansemond people joined other Native nations. Some assimilated into US society but many kept their tribe's culture and traditions alive.

In 2022 Cross Swamp was returned to the Nansemond Indian Nation of Virginia. The land was sold to a conservation group that worked with federal agencies to return the land to the Nansemond Nation.

In 2020 Native American peoples protest at Black Hills Regional Park in South Dakota.

The Land Back movement is helping bring more stolen lands back to Native nations, letting them be stewards of the land again. Native nations and peoples are standing up for their sacred places and freedom to live by their spiritual traditions.

Glossary

archaeological: referring to the scientific study of material remains (such as tools, pottery, jewelry, stone walls, and monuments) of past human life and activities

assimilate: when people change or are forced to change their traditions and customs to become part of a different group

burial site: an area of land where people have been buried

desecrate: to treat a sacred place or thing with disrespect

loot: to steal or take by force

monument: a building, structure, or site that is of historical importance or interest

preserve: to keep something the same or to prevent it from being damaged

remains: body parts and bones of people who have died

repatriate: to restore or return to the country of origin, allegiance, or citizenship

steward: someone who carefully and responsibly looks after something

time immemorial: thousands of years before European settlers came to the land that is now the US

Learn More

Bellanger DeGroat, Cayla. *Indigenous Cultures Today: Protecting Native Families and Practicing Cultural Traditions*. Minneapolis: Lerner Publications, 2025.

Britannica Kids: Indigenous Land Back Movement
https://kids.britannica.com/students/assembly/view/281435

Britannica Kids: NAGPRA
https://kids.britannica.com/kids/article/NAGPRA/635371

Bruegl, Heather. *What Is Land Back?* Ann Arbor, MI: Cherry Lake, 2024.

Doerfler, Jill, and Matthew J. Martinez. *Deb Haaland: First Native American Cabinet Secretary*. Minneapolis: Lerner Publications, 2023.

Kiddle: Nansemond Facts for Kids
https://kids.kiddle.co/Nansemond

National Park Service: First Stories
https://www.nps.gov/deto/learn/historyculture/first-stories.htm

Washburne, Sophie. *The Story of the Native American Rights Movement*. Buffalo: Cavendish Square, 2024.

Index

Photo Acknowledgments

Image credits: Wiskerke/Alamy, p. 5; Jeffrey Isaac Greenberg 2+/Alamy, p. 7; Steven Love/Alamy, p. 8; Todd Strand/Alamy, p. 12; DEA/A. DAGLI ORTI/Getty Images, p. 13; Bettmann/Getty Images, p. 15; Heritage Art/ Heritage Images via Getty Images, p. 17; Europa Press via Getty Images, p. 18; California Native American Heritage Commission, p. 21; CHANDAN KHANNA/AFP via Getty Images, p. 22; Photo Beto/Getty Images, p. 23; AP Photo/Juneau Empire, Michael Penn, p. 24; MicheleVacchiano/Getty Images, p. 25; AP Photo/David Goldman, p. 27; AP Photo/Matt Rourke, p. 28; Micah Garen/Getty Images, p. 29.Design elements: kiwihug/Unsplash; Miloje/ Shutterstock; Archiwiz/Shutterstock; mikesj11/Shutterstock.

Cover: Forgem/Shutterstock; VETOCHKA/Shutterstock.